VIENNA

Fountains of the Maidens are what give Schönbrunn Palace (where both Marie Antoinette and Napoleon's son lived as children) its name, for Schönbrunn means "beautiful fountain."

VIENNA

by KEIICHI UCHIGAKI

Published by
KODANSHA INTERNATIONAL LTD.
Tokyo, Japan & Palo Alto, Calif., U.S.A.

Distributed in the British Commonwealth (excluding Canada and the Far East) by Ward Lock & Company Ltd., London and Sydney; in Continental Europe by Boxerbooks, Inc., Zurich; and in the Far East by Japan Publications Trading Co., C.P.O. Box 722, Tokyo. Published by Kodansha International Ltd., 2-12-21, Otowa, Bunkyo-ku, Tokyo, Japan and Kodansha International/USA, Ltd., 599 College Avenue, Palo Alto, California 94306. Copyright © 1970, by Kodansha International Ltd. All rights reserved. Printed in Japan.

Library of Congress Catalog Card No. 75-100625
S.B.N. 87011-107-8; J.B.C. No. 0325-781330-2361
First edition, 1970
Second printing, 1970

VIENNA

The City of Music

Vienna today is the capital of a democratic, federal republic whose total population is around seven million; a century ago, she was the capital of a vast, sprawling empire that was not the first (and probably will not be the last) to claim that the sun never set on its boundaries. At the same time that she was administering, or failing to administer, this huge and rickety empire, Vienna played host to the most sparkling collection of musical geniuses the world has ever known. It is generally accepted that Vienna went through two successive golden ages, one under the Empress Maria Theresa, and the other just before World War I, under Emperor Franz Joseph. The character of these two periods differed considerably in accordance with the atmosphere fostered by the two monarchs and influenced not only the music but also the literature, theater, and architecture.

The aristocratic Golden Age of Maria Theresa developed into the more free-spirited, bourgeois Golden Age of Franz Joseph. But throughout these golden ages the unwieldy empire of which Vienna was the heart was feeling the pangs of imminent extinction. By the end of World War I, the body was dead, but the heart continued to beat. And it beats still—in three-quarter time, of course.

VIENNA 🌿

It was inevitable that a great city should rise on or near the site of present-day Vienna, for it lies where two ancient trade routes cross: the waterway (now known as the Danube) that links east with west, and the land road from the Adriatic to the Baltic, linking north and south. Over these two great highways passed the migrations of the most varied people, some of whom came to see and conquer, others to trade, still others to settle down by the banks of the river and perhaps be conquered unless they succeeded in defending themselves.

Vienna's story actually begins long before recorded history. The most ancient object that has yet been found in the neighborhood of Vienna is the so-called Venus of Willendorf, a small female figure in stone that is generally conceded to be a fertility symbol. It dates from Paleolithic times, some twenty thousand years ago. Objects have also been found in Vienna that man fashioned during the Neolithic period as well as during the Bronze Age, which would seem to suggest that during all that time Vienna was continuously occupied. With the establishment of the Romans in the Danube basin toward the close of the first century B.C., the region entered recorded history for the first time.

But before that was to happen, the site of present-day Vienna became a Celtic settlement, and it was these Celts whom the Roman legionaries encountered when they came marching north and east. They succeeded in subjugating the tribes south of the Danube but not those to the north: the beautiful blue Danube (which perhaps *was* blue in those days) thus became the northernmost boundary of the Roman occupation of central Europe in the first century B.C. The Romans enlarged the Celtic settlement that was there, making it a *castrum* for the Thirteenth Legion, and giving it the

Latin name of Vindobona: *vino* means "wine"; *bona*, "good." Vindobona lay snugly within the precincts of what is now called the Innere Stadt, or Inner City, of Vienna, bounded on three sides by the Ring and on the fourth by a man-made canal branching off from the Danube. As Vienna is the heart of Austria, the Innere Stadt is the heart of Vienna; it is there that most of the chief monuments lie, and many of her grandest shops, restaurants, and hotels. But the Innere Stadt is a long way in time, if not in space, from the Roman frontier post of Vindobona.

Many writers have pointed out the deep debt Vienna owes these conquering Romans, who brought to the city the gifts of their far more advanced civilization. Perhaps even more important than the roads they laid down were the walls they built up, for behind defensive walls Vienna was to be called upon, many centuries in the future, to protect herself (and indeed all of Europe on the other side of her) against mighty, seemingly invincible Turkish armies. And perhaps even more important than either roads or walls was the law that the Romans brought with them. Sons of unlettered tribesmen were soon to be able to say, and to say with pride, "*civis Romanus sum*"; during the second century, the *Pax Romana* enabled them to cultivate not only the grape that the Romans brought but also the arts of peace. Vienna gained far more than she lost with the Romanization of Vindobona.

But, as Vienna herself was to learn one day, no empire lasts forever: at the moment of its greatest expansion, the seed of decay is already planted. The impregnable fortress of Carnuntum was destroyed by the Germans in the fourth century A.D., and hegemony in the Danube passed to Vindobona. The eminence was, however, only a temporary one. The empire was crumbling; the Goths, the

1. *Augarten Palais* is now headquar-▶
ters of the Wiener Sängerknaben,
Vienna's ancient and world-famous
boys' choir.

VIENNA 🪶

Vandals, and the Huns were to have their brief—and terrible—day.
By the end of the fifth century, the last Roman had fled from Austria,
and Vindobona was exposed to the savagery of the Barbarian tribes.
It had the doubtful honor of being raided by Attila himself and his
Huns.

For the next few centuries, the Danube plains were the scene
of an extraordinary mingling of tribes and races from east, north,
and west (Magyars, Slavs, Teutons, Bajuvars), and of the confron-
tations among them. At the same time, despite the warlike incursions
of the various tribes, Christianity was making its efforts to become
the one and only religion of the region. Toward the middle of the
eighth century, the Church of St. Rupert was founded in what is now
Vienna and an abbey was established in Salzburg.

A few years later, the future of Vienna was determined in a
more decisive manner in quite another place: King Charles of the
Franks, better known to history as Charlemagne, was crowned
Roman Emperor of the West in Rome in the year 800. It was a title
that had long fallen into disuse: for several centuries, the only
Roman emperor had been the one who sat on the imperial throne
at Constantinople. It was during Charlemagne's Eastern March
(the *Mark im Ostland*) that the Vienna area was incorporated, and
the city itself reappears in the records as Wenia when, around 880,
the Franks engaged the Magyars there. In the year 907 the Magyars
were successful in their determined efforts to destroy the Frankish
Eastern March—but only temporarily.

For, but five years after the Magyar victory, a son was born to
King Henry I of Germany (called the Fowler) and his second
wife, Matilda. Christened Otto, the boy was destined to restore
German hegemony to the district: on the Lechfeld in 955 Otto

10

3. *Vienna Octet* is composed of members of the Vienna Philharmonic, an orchestra of world renown that gave its first performance in 1842.

2. *Konzerthaus* is one of the two largest concert halls in Vienna; the other is the Musikverein-saal; and both are used alternately during Vienna's famous Festival Week (*Festwochen*).

4. *Vienna* is a city where it is difficult to escape the sounds of music; here a quartet entertains at Schrammel's, a winehouse named after Josef Schrammel, who was one of the first to combine music with wine for his customers.

inflicted so stunning a defeat on the Magyars that they were forced to retreat to Hungary. The Ostmark was accordingly reestablished, and less than seven years later Otto was in Rome, where he was crowned as the first of the Holy Roman emperors, he and the pope having exchanged vows of fidelity. Although Otto's reign was not so glorious as that of Charlemagne had been, and although he himself was virtually illiterate, he encouraged scholars and artists, and there is no question that his loyalty to the Roman church must account at least in part for the fact that some ninety percent of the population of Austria today, despite the efforts of the Protestants, is Roman Catholic.

It is now that the Babenbergs enter the story of Vienna, where they were to remain firmly entrenched for the next two centuries and a half. The first Babenberg known to history was a ninth century count in Grapfeld who bore the unlikely name of Poppo. One of his presumed descendants was Count Luitpold, or Leopold, who in 976 was appointed by Otto II (son of the first Otto) to be margrave of the Ostmark—which meant Austria, which meant Vienna. The fortunes of the country and its rulers were, until their extinction, inseparable.

The Babenbergs were an able family, industrious and imaginative, and under their rule Austria prospered. The Niederaltaich Annals of 1030 mention a town called Wiennis, which can surely be no other than Vienna, so presumably it was under the rule of the third margrave, Adalbert, that the town began to grow again, although it was not to become the capital until over a century later. However, the great walls were being built that formed part of the Ostmark's line of defense against invasion from both east and north, while outside those walls rose the first structure in Vienna dedicated to

15

St. Stephen. It was a Romanesque church (destined to be destroyed by fire in 1276), and around it, as frequently happened in those early days, rose houses and shops. The Innere Stadt, the heart of Vienna, was expanding—and the city's love for its patron saint found its first artistic expression.

Leopold III (the Pious) is generally considered to be the most outstanding of the eight Babenberg margraves. He built a great castle, founded a number of monasteries, and made a strategic marriage to the daughter of the German king, Henry IV, thus setting a precedent for the manner in which the Austrian empire was later to expand so phenomenally. Leopold's nephew, Henry II, was the last of the family to bear the title of margrave, for during his reign the region, known now as Austria, was made a hereditary duchy by the redoubtable Holy Roman emperor, Frederick I, better known as Barbarossa. This elevation of Austria from a margraviate to a duchy was compensation for Henry's renunciation of Bavaria. Henry made two marriages that helped to consolidate the position of the Babenbergs—and of Austria—in medieval Europe. His first wife was the widow of Henry the Proud, duke of Saxony and Bavaria, and his second was the daughter of Emperor Manuel of Byzantium. He is known to history as Henry Jasomirgott because of his partiality for the oath, *Ja, so mir Gott helfe*—"Yes, if God helps me." From in front of St. Stephen's Cathedral, in present-day Vienna, there goes a short street called Jasomirgottstrasse—perhaps in recognition of the fact that it was this Henry who made Vienna his capital.

After the death of the last of the Babenbergs, Duke Frederick II, who was killed giving battle to King Bela IV of Hungary (Frederick was called the Quarrelsome), there followed an unhappy period in the life of Vienna, known now as the Interregnum, known then as the Years of Terror. Emperor quarreled with pope as to who should succeed the Babenbergs, but with the death of the emperor in 1250 Vienna was forced to accept King Ottakar of Bohemia, who contributed heavily toward the rebuilding of the city after the disastrous fire of 1262. But Ottakar's reign was not to be a long one. A certain Count Rudolph, who took his surname from his castle at Habsburg, was elected King of the Germans in 1273, and one of his first tasks was to rid Austria of the Bohemian king, who had refused to recognize his sovereignty. The two monarchs met on the plain of Marchfeld, east of Vienna, and in 1278 Ottakar's army was thoroughly routed and he himself slain. Rudolph was now free to do what he liked with Austria, and Vienna was soon to become the seat of a dynasty that was destined to endure until 1918.

The castle of Habsburg, or Habichtsburg ("Hawk's Castle"), or—derisively—Habenichtsburg ("Have Not Castle"), was built in 1028 on the Aar near where it meets the Rhine. The founder of the house of Habsburg was presumably Count Guntram the Rich, but by the time Rudolph was elected German king, the family was not noted for its wealth, although Rudolph had supported the emperors Frederick II and Conrad IV and had in turn been rewarded by them. Even before his election, he had begun to follow the policy that was to become Habsburg practice: he married his daughters to the dukes of Saxe-Lauenburg and of upper Bavaria, thus ensuring the support of his sons-in-law in electing him German king. He also made several compromises in order to win the support of the pope. Rudolph, according to contemporary descriptions, was tall and slender, with long legs and long, slim fingers; by nature he was grave and temperate, and everyone seemed to agree that he had both high intelligence and great strength of character. That he was ambitious became obvious once he had secured the election. Not only did he destroy Ottakar and take over Austria but he also forced the count of upper Burgundy to give him some land and the citizens of Berne to pay him tribute. He seems, in all, a likely sort of person to have set the house of Habsburg on its path to grandeur.

In 1282 he made his two sons princes of the empire, investing them with the duchies of Austria and Styria, but the following year he decided that dual sovereignty was not desirable. He therefore gave both Austria and Styria to his elder son, Albert, and solaced Rudolph, the younger, with money. This question of inheritance was to plague the greedy Habsburgs in the future and was to account, in fact, for one of their temporary declines.

Before his death Rudolph tried and failed to ensure the election of his son Albert as German king, but some years later Albert managed to defeat the elected king in battle and to win the ensuing election. Once again the pope withheld recognition until after Albert had made certain concessions. True to Habsburg tradition, Albert succeeded, in 1306, in securing the Bohemian throne for his son Rudolph. Two years later he was murdered by his nephew, whose inheritance he had appropriated.

The fourteenth century was a momentous one in the history of Vienna and the Habsburgs. There was a great fire in 1327, ten years later a devastating plague of locusts, in another ten years an earthquake, and the year after that a major epidemic of cholera. On the other side of the ledger was the important fact that the University of Vienna was founded in 1365, while work on the new cathedral continued throughout the century. As for the Habsburgs themselves, they pursued their expansionist policy. Carinthia,

South Tyrol, and Vorarlberg fell into their hands; then the eccentric Margaret Maultasch, Duchess of Tyrol, made over her lands and castle to Rudolph IV. Not long after that, the Habsburgs acquired Istria and parts of Friuli, the Bregenzerwald and Feldkirch, Trieste and more of Vorarlberg.

The following century, despite family squabbles, saw no weakening in the Habsburgs' determination to increase their land holdings. Opinion appears to be divided as to whether or not it was King Matthias Corvinus of Hungary who said, *"Bella gerant alii; tu, felix Austria, nube."* ("Let others wage war; you, happy Austria, marry.") And if it was indeed the king, opinion is further divided as to whether he was referring to Frederick III or to his son Maximilian, for while it was the latter who married the heiress of Charles the Bold, thus placing in Habsburg hands the huge holdings of the Duchy of Burgundy, it was the former who arranged the marriage.

The event was characteristic of Frederick's way of going to work, of getting what he wanted—and what he wanted was not to be a wise, just, or energetic ruler but rather to increase Habsburg holdings and add luster to the Habsburg name. It is on his splendid tomb in St. Stephen's that the famous letters appear, letters that Frederick was also in the habit of inscribing in his books: A.E.I.O.U. The customary Latin version is *Austriae est imperare orbi universo*: "It is for Austria to rule the whole world."

When he was twenty-five, Frederick was chosen to be German king, and three years later began secret negotiations with the pope aimed at securing the crown of the Holy Roman Empire for himself. By the time he was thirty-seven, he had succeeded. In 1452, he was married to Leonora of Portugal in Rome and three days later was crowned emperor by Pope Nicholas V. In return, he pledged that

19

the German people would remain loyal to the papacy, despite country-wide agitation against Rome. That he was more interested in his family than his people seems evident from the devious and painstaking care by which he set about capturing the imperial crown while doing nothing to counter the growing threat from the Turks, who, having taken Constantinople, were now looking with aggressive eyes toward the west—toward Budapest and then Vienna.

The first Habsburg emperor now set about the delicate task of marrying his son to the daughter of the Duke of Burgundy, but the negotiations fell through when the emperor declined to grant the duke the title of king. The emperor was content to wait. Within four years the duke was dead, and his daughter married Maximilian, bringing into the Habsburg fold the vast holdings of the Duchy of Burgundy, including Flanders, Holland, Zeeland, Franche-Comté, and Luxemburg.

Yet the man who was capable of securing all this for his family was incapable of defending his capital. When King Matthias of Hungary attacked Vienna, Frederick fled, leaving Matthias in possession of the city until his death in 1490. Matthias was, by all accounts, a far abler man than Frederick in every way; he merely lacked the Habsburg preoccupation with Habsburg status.

Frederick's son and heir, Maximilian, seems to have spent most of his time defending and attempting to increase the area under Habsburg rule. In this he was a true son of his house. His son Philip he married to Juana the Mad (of Castile and Aragon), and then his grandson Ferdinand to Anne of Bohemia. His was also a valiant and intrepid fighter—"the last of the knights," he has been called—and more than once barely escaped with his life from the battlefield.

Maximilian found time to write a number of books on varied subjects, including autobiographical notes, and Vienna, although he preferred not to live there, remains in his debt, for he reorganized the university and founded what is now the Austrian National Library. He is also responsible for the Vienna Hofkapelle and Boys' Choir. It is not a poor record for a man who was continually making and breaking alliances, quarreling and fighting with his fellow monarchs, arranging dynastic marriages, and envisaging grandiose schemes for the glorification of the Habsburg name. At one time, after he had quarreled with Pope Julius II, he considered putting the tiara of Rome on his own head!

Philip predeceased him, bequeathing the title of King of Spain to his six-year-old son Charles, a title the boy was not to assume for another ten years. In addition to Spain itself and the vast Spanish empire, which was soon to include Mexico and Peru, the boy inherited Burgundy from his father and Austria, a little later, from his grandfather. In 1520 he was crowned Holy Roman emperor, and in the same year acquired the Duchy of Württemberg, thus consolidating his Austrian holdings, which he then gave to his brother Ferdinand. There were now two distinct Habsburg branches, one ruling from Spain and one in Austria.

When Charles implemented his long-felt desire to abdicate all his many thrones, that of Spain passed to his son while that of the Holy Roman Empire went to his brother Ferdinand. The coming years were not to be very happy ones for either branch: the Spanish Habsburgs had ambitious French kings to contend with, while the Austrians were beleaguered by the Turks from the east and by Protestants from the west. When, in fact, Ferdinand reached Wiener Neustadt to take possession of his Austrian inheritance, he was greeted by a Protestant rebellion emanating from Vienna. The emperor, devoutly Catholic, executed the leaders of the rebellion and exiled the others who had taken part in it, and what had formerly been an elected municipal government now became one appointed by the crown.

Even this small measure of peace was rudely broken three years later when Suleiman the Magnificent, sultan of Turkey, brought his army to the gates of Vienna and laid siege to the city. The siege was eventually lifted, but the Turks overran Hungary, carrying off numerous captives, and some years later succeeded in annexing central and southern Hungary, which they used as a base for raid after raid into Austria during the century and a half of their Hungarian occupation.

To counter growing Protestantism in Austria, Ferdinand invited the Jesuits to come to Vienna, thus inaugurating the Counter Reformation, which was to have so strong an influence not only on the people of the city but also on its very face, its art and its music. The Jesuits indicated, at the very start, that they understood that there was a difference between Austria and Spain and that the stake was not the way to win Viennese friends—or even to influence them. They decided, instead, to erect theaters for the performance of specially written religious plays. If it was their intention to amuse the Viennese into forsaking Protestantism, they succeeded spectacularly well—although it took them a long time. Today about ninety percent of the population of the city is Catholic.

Ferdinand's immediate successors—his son and his two grandsons—took little interest in public life, and because of the absence of a forceful and energetic emperor, conditions in the empire deteriorated rapidly within the half-century that followed Ferdinand's death. However, the new emperor, Ferdinand II, who came to the throne in 1619, was not only a staunch Catholic, he was also a man of energy and determination. It was he who ruthlessly put down the Protestant revolt in Bohemia, regaining some of the Habsburgs' lost prestige, and he also who decreed that only Catholics could be citizens. As a result, a number of Protestant families left the country.

And as a result of Ferdinand's action in Bohemia, there followed a series of wars in Europe known as the Thirty Years' War (1618–48), in which most important European countries found themselves involved in one way or another.

In the year of Ferdinand's birth (1578), a ceremony was held to mark the completion of the North Tower of St. Stephen's Cathedral, and two years later the famous Spanish Riding School was established—two events of great local significance. The accession of Ferdinand III to the throne, in 1637, may be said to have planted the seed for the great flowering of Viennese musical genius that was still in the future, for Ferdinand was the first of four monarchs who were not only patrons of music and musicians themselves but composers as well.

By the end of Ferdinand's reign, in 1657, the threat to Habsburg autocracy posed by the Reformation had ended, and the empire was once again firmly under central control. Vienna was fortunate in that respect, for she was soon to be menaced by two major disasters. The first, which occurred in the year 1679, was one of the most disastrous of a series of plagues that had ravaged the city from time to time for centuries. According to one account, half the population died in 1679; others estimated the number of deaths to be a hundred thousand, or more.

VIENNA ❧

In any case, there were so many dead bodies that there were not enough living people left to bury them; convicts were released from prison on condition that they take on the onerous task. Everyone who could afford to left the city; the emperor himself went to Mariazell in Styria. By 1682 life in the city was sufficiently restored for the emperor to command the construction of the famous Pestsäule (Plague Memorial) on the Graben. It was to be designed jointly by Fischer von Erlach the elder, court architect, and Lodovico Burnacini, court theater designer, and was to be entirely in white marble.

But before this most baroque of baroque monuments was even off the drawing boards, Vienna was faced by a greater crisis than the plague. The Turkish empire, then at the height of its power, saw a Europe weakened and ravaged by long years of war. It seemed ripe for conquest, and all the more so as the dynastic squabbles that had prompted the wars would tend to prevent the various Christian nations from forming an alliance against the Moslem Turks. The sultan Mohammed IV had signed a peace treaty with the emperor Leopold I that was to expire in 1684. The sultan determined to launch his attack while the treaty was still in force. Accordingly, he dispatched an army of nearly three hundred thousand men, under the command of his grand vizier, Kara Mustafa, to lay siege to Vienna—for Vienna's role, historically and strategically, has been to serve as a kind of outpost on the Islamic east.

When the Turkish army was sighted, in the summer of 1683, Vienna was thrown into panic. The emperor promptly left his capital, accompanied by most of his court. More than fifty thousand Viennese fled their beleagured city, leaving a defensive force of around fifteen thousand to face the Turkish horde.

The commander of the garrison, Count Starhemberg, rejected Kara Mustafa's offer of peace under Islam and the sultan and prepared for the siege. By mid-July the city was wholly surrounded, and the Turkish army began its slow encroachment on the city walls. On September 4, the Turks succeeded in forcing a hole in one of the walls, and troops began flowing into the city with the word "Allah" on their lips. If Vienna were to fall to the Turks, all of Europe might well fall with her. But the Viennese, although they lost two hundred men, managed to repel the invaders.

Vienna, for the moment, was saved, but the situation was still desperate. Aside from the threat posed by the huge Turkish army, the people within the besieged city were suffering horribly from hunger, thirst, and disease. If help did not come soon, Vienna was surely doomed, and with the collapse of the Austrian empire, the Turks would find the road to Venice and the west a far easier one.

But help *was* coming. Twenty thousand Poles under their king, Jan Sobieski, joined twenty-five thousand Austrian soldiers led by Duke Charles of Lorraine. On the decisive day, September 12, Starhemberg coordinated his garrison with the relieving troops; the battle began at dawn, and by four in the afternoon the Turkish army had begun to retreat. Soon they were fleeing east toward Hungary. Vienna had been saved and the road to the west closed.

Work began again on the Pestsäule. At the base knelt a statue of the emperor, Leopold I (who had returned to Vienna from his stay in the country). He was shown being crowned by an angel, while Faith was represented in relief as triumphant over Pestilence. Above rose a great bank of clouds, on which rested a column topped by the Trinity and the Nine Choirs of Angels. And all done in the whitest of marble. The day of Vienna's greatness was dawning;

and the "year of the Turks" was also the year that Vienna's first coffee house, the first one in the Western world, opened.

The period following the Turkish rout was a busy one for the city. For one thing, it had seen the arrival of Johann Bernhard Fischer, later ennobled as von Erlach, fresh from his studies of baroque architecture in Rome and more than ready to serve the newly returned Viennese aristocrats in helping to make their city conform to the prevailing architectural mood in Europe. There appears to be no certain derivation for the word "baroque," save that it is a French adaptation of either the Portugese *baeroco* or the Spanish *barrueco*, both of which mean a rough, irregularly shaped pearl; beyond that, the etymology is uncertain. And how, in any case, did it come to refer to the wide variety of fine arts and the architectural styles that decorated the face of Europe during the sixteenth, seventeenth, and early eighteenth centuries? These buildings are neither rough nor irregularly shaped—as a glance at any of Fischer von Erlach's constructions will demonstrate.

They do, however, express an exuberant pleasure in the drama that life is capable of—and so are eminently suitable to the emotional climate of Vienna. Two architects—Fischer von Erlach and Johann Lukas von Hildebrandt—were kept so busy in those postwar years that by 1720 Vienna boasted over two hundred palaces, villas, and churches in the baroque style. Vienna's streets, wrote Lady Mary Wortley Montague in 1716, are "very close, and so narrow, one cannot observe the fine fronts of the palaces, though many of them very well deserve observation, being truly magnificent. ... " Lady Mary, who had seen the finest houses of England and had traveled widely on the continent, may, without prejudice, be considered a worthy judge of the "magnificent."

26

Fischer von Erlach reached the summit of his art in the construction of the Karlskirche, which, like the Pestsäule, rose out of the dead bones of victims of the plague. This particular one was at its most virulent in 1713, and that was when the then emperor, Charles VI, determined to offer a church to his patron saint, St. Charles Borromeo. Fischer von Erlach submitted the winning design. This magnificent and flamboyant construction was completed within sixteen years. The speed of baroque (as compared with the slow pace of Gothic, which often required several centuries to build a church) is another of its characteristics. Baroque had no time for marble; it made use of stucco, which it could fashion into whatever fantastic shape it chose. The palaces went up so fast, in fact, that soon there was no room left in the Innere Stadt, and the rich began to build their dwellings on greener and airier fields outside the city walls. Much further out rose Fischer's grandiose imperial palace of Schönbrunn—"beautiful fountain" (though less grandiose in reality than in the original intention of the architect); nearer the city, Hildebrandt was working on the Belvedere for Prince Eugene of Savoy.

The Belvedere was only one of many baroque palaces that Prince Eugene commissioned in the course of his strenuous career. Although a foreigner by birth, he faithfully served three Austrian emperors, both on clamorous fields of battle and at the gilt tables of diplomacy, and he was handsomely rewarded. He becomes, in fact, a kind of symbol of this period in Viennese history, as baroque in his own way as the palaces he commissioned. "Leopold was my father; Joseph, my brother; and Charles, my master," he is reported to have said of the three emperors for whom he fought. At the end of his life he had the satisfaction—if it was indeed a satisfaction to him—of seeing the capital of a small duchy become

VIENNA ✣

the capital of a huge empire that sprawled from the Mediterranean up to the North Sea.

During those three reigns Vienna was not just building the airy palaces that lend such grace to the city. She was putting the Turk in his place—Istanbul, to be exact; and she was recovering much of the land in eastern Europe that Turkish armies had occupied. At the same time, she was attempting to combat the power of Bourbon France, which the Habsburgs had always seen as a threat. At this task Prince Eugene was at his happiest, for his mother had been forced to flee the French court in disgrace, and he himself had been refused a commission in the army of Louis XIV.

There was also the War of the Spanish Succession to be attended to, for in the year 1700 the last male Spanish Habsburg had died without issue. It was Leopold's intention to put his elder son, Joseph, on the throne of Austria, and Charles, his younger son, on the Spanish throne. Louis XIV had quite another idea: he wanted to see a Bourbon on the throne of Spain. With Spain went the still enormous Spanish empire, including Belgium, the Netherlands and much of what is now Italy as well as colonies in America, Africa, and the Philippines. It was a prize worth fighting for—and for ten years the powers of Europe did exactly that. Here Prince Eugene fought brilliantly by the side of the Duke of Marlborough, and Austria not only won Bavaria and northern Italy but looked as though she was, with England's help, going to win Spain as well.

Then, in 1711, Joseph, who had come to the throne in 1705 on the death of Leopold, died—and England, fearing a union of Austria and Spain under a single monarch, decided to make a separate peace with France. Austria now had no choice but to follow suit and in 1714 signed a treaty by which the huge Spanish territories that had until that time been Habsburg now became Bourbon.

There was still one other major task for Prince Eugene to accomplish in the service of his masters, and that was to secure the Austrian succession. Emperor Charles VI had only one son, who died in infancy, and two daughters. Even before the birth of the elder, in 1717, he had been haunted by the possibility that the Austrian Habsburgs would die out just as the Spanish line had done. He therefore promulgated a family ruling called the Pragmatic Sanction, by the terms of which lands under Habsburg rule could be bequeathed to only one heir and could be ruled by a woman if there was no male heir to assume power.

By general agreement, however, most countries of Europe at that time subscribed to certain provisions of the Salic Law, an early medieval Frankish compendium one of whose provisons was that daughters may not inherit land. Fearful that the law might be invoked to deprive a daughter of his of the crown, Charles began delicate negotiations with the chief powers of Europe to secure their agreement that, should he die without male issue, they would accept his daughter as heiress to the House of Austria. Thanks to the tireless efforts of Prince Eugene, agreement was finally wrested from France, England, Prussia, Spain, Russia, Holland, and Denmark, among others. That Charles had to make concessions of various kinds in order to ensure the approval of the powers he did not consider too high a price to pay—and so the Viennese stage was set for the brilliant, if stormy, entry, in 1740, of twenty-three-year-old Maria Theresa, accompanied by her consort, François of Lorraine, as Holy Roman emperor and empress. Although they were co-regents, and although the house was thenceforward known as that of Habsburg-Lorraine, it was Maria Theresa who wielded the real power; for the Habsburgs, as history had repeatedly shown, were a more tenacious family than most.

Yet one of the first things that befell Maria Theresa was the loss of her wealthy, industrial duchies of Silesia. Prussia had long felt it had a claim to these duchies, and when Frederick II (sometimes known as "the Great") became king (in the same year that Maria Theresa ascended the throne of Austria) he decided to act. He immediately sent an ambassador to Vienna, offering assistance to Maria Theresa in return for Silesia; his request was haughtily refused, and Frederick, having already made preparations, began an immediate invasion. Although his father had been a signatory to the Pragmatic Sanction, Frederick declared it invalid insofar as Silesia was concerned, and for some years the two monarchs squabbled, with the other powers of Europe either taking sides or marching armies eastward in the hope of acquiring some of the spoils of a vanquished empire. In the end, Maria Theresa had to acquiesce to the loss of Silesia, but, largely through her strength of character and her obvious goodness, rallied her people and armies behind her and eventually succeeded in guarding the rest of her inheritance. She also had the intelligence to recognize the very real abilities of Prince von Kaunitz, employing him first as ambassador and second appointing him her imperial chancellor, a position of tremendous power and importance. Kaunitz never failed her, managing to effect military alliances against Prussia with both France and Russia.

Vienna, meanwhile, under Maria Theresa's intelligent and, on the whole, benevolent reign, prospered despite the sporadic wars on which the empire embarked during those four decades. New buildings kept going up, many of them to house the various new institutions that Maria Theresa established, such as the Theresianum College. One of her major efforts was directed at overcoming the disadvantages her sprawling empire suffered in the diversity of its peoples and languages. She sought to establish a uniform administrative code, and could, in fact, almost be called a tolerant monarch—so long as no attempt was made to diminish her absolute authority.

Her reign, however, derives its chief glory from the fact that with it Western music not only came to fruition but reached heights it has never achieved since. The year 1762 was a crucial one, for it saw not only the first performance of Gluck's *Orfeo ed Euridice* at Vienna's old Burgtheater but also the patronage by Prince Nicholas Esterhazy (called the Magnificent) of Franz Joseph Haydn, so that the composer would thenceforward be free of financial worries, as well as the reception at Schönbrunn Palace by the imperial family of a six-year-old musical prodigy named Wolfgang Amadeus Mozart. If it is hard to imagine Gluck, Haydn, and Mozart living and working in the same city at the same time, it is harder still to imagine the little Mozart boy slipping on one of the polished floors at Schönbrunn and being helped to his feet by a little archduchess, hardly older than himself. "How kind you are!" he said to her. "When I am grown up, I shall marry you." Her reply, unfortunately, is lost to history, but not her name: it was Marie Antoinette, who was one day to be queen of France—and one day not.

In 1765, Emperor Francis died, and his son became emperor and co-regent with Maria Theresa, but still it was she who continued to wield the greater power, although Joseph II, as he grew more experienced at the trade of being an emperor, grew more insistent upon being allowed to practice it. Then too, as she grew older,

VIENNA 𝒴

Maria Theresa found that the demands of family and dynasty occupied more and more of her time. She had sixteen children (ten
of whom survived her) and tried to make for them brilliant matches
that would enhance the Habsburg name. Perhaps with none did she
succeed so well (or, as it turned out, so ill) as with Marie Antoinette.
When she sent her to France to be the wife of the dauphin, she
cautioned her to be polite to her husband's grandfather's mistresses,
so that relations between the two courts should not be strained,
for Louis XV was as absolute a Bourbon as Maria Theresa a Habsburg. When she lay dying, her son and heir, visiting her deathbed,
said to her, "I fear you are uncomfortable." "I am comfortable
enough to die," she replied—and did, thus ending the first, aristocratic Golden Age of Viennese culture.

The reign of her son Joseph, however well-intentioned and revolutionary, was very nearly disastrous for the Habsburg empire. In
part, it was Maria Theresa's own fault, for when he was a boy she
commanded that he should be educated as though he were being
amused. As a result, what real education he acquired came from
Voltaire and the French Encyclopedists; and as a result of *that*
came Joseph's clear vision of himself as an enlightened and pro-
gressive monarch, supreme in the state, but ruled by reason, of
whose reasonableness he himself was to be the sole judge.

With the death of his mother he was free to inaugurate all the
reforms he deemed essential to an enlightened state, and some of
them, such as the abolition of torture, were admirable indeed. The
French influence he had undergone, combined with his membership
in the Free Masonry, led him to attempt benevolent action for his
people, but several factors militated against his success. For one
thing, there were simply too many reforms; and for another, they

came too fast: no one was quite ready for the breadth and speed of them. A third disadvantage was Joseph's lack of tact: he managed to antagonize most of the people he needed to put his reforms into effect. Toward the close of his ten-year reign the empire was in chaos and on the verge of bankruptcy.

Yet never, anywhere in the world, had there been such a musical decade as in Vienna between 1780 and 1790. Joseph himself was a partron and lover of music, and not only did the nobles follow suit but, when he made the Burgtheater into a national theater, the bourgeoisie began for the first time to participate in musical activities on an equal footing. There were musical evenings in almost all the great palaces of the city, from Schönbrunn down, and members of the nobility often performed in the orchestra. Joseph's ten-year reign coincided with the last ten years of Mozart's life— years that saw the composition of his great operas and much of his finest orchestral music. It was during this time that the *Magic Flute*, musically anticipating the ideals of the French Revolution, was presented—with the author-producer Schikaneder also singing and dancing the role of Papageno. Maria Theresa's physician had been a man named van Swieten, whose son Gottfried gave musical mornings every Sunday at his apartment in the Renngasse. Mozart was a frequent visitor. This picture is perhaps as characteristic as any of that glorious yet unfortunate decade in Vienna when Maria Theresa's eldest surviving son was Holy Roman emperor.

On Joseph's death, his younger brother Leopold ascended the throne for a short two-year reign, and his chief efforts were directed at restoring domestic stability and the international prestige of the Habsburgs. In this he was largely successful, and he was successful also in avoiding any armed conflict with the new revolutionary government of France (which, a year after his own death, would put his younger sister to the guillotine). If it is odd to conjecture how different was life in the two great European capitals that year of 1792, with the guillotine working overtime in Paris and the harpsichord in Vienna, it is even odder to realize that while Leopold sat decorously at a musical evening at Schönbrunn, his younger sister, soon to be the widow Capet, huddled in confinement in Paris, wondering how much longer her head would remain attached to her body. The oddity would shortly become odder still—and then would not be odd at all, for with the beginning of the next reign, France would find herself at war with Austria, a war that was not to end until the defeat of Napoleon and the Congress of Vienna.

Emperor Francis, who succeeded his father Leopold, played first violin in the imperial string quartet but soon found other employment, as did his field-marshal who played the viola. Save for brief periods of relative peace, Vienna—for the next two decades— was to find herself the capital of an empire at war, first with the revolutionary government of France, and then with France's master and emperor and one of history's greatest military geniuses (if the two words are not incompatible). Twice during those twenty years the city was occupied by the conqueror, and the empire of which she was the capital was chopped up until very little of it was left. Napoleon installed himself at Schönbrunn and demanded the hand of Francis's daughter, Marie Louise. Their son, whose first title was King of Rome and whose second was Napoleon II, died at Schönbrunn at the age of twenty-one, known merely as the Duke of Reichstadt. The son of the "great" Napoleon had in the end to give precedence to the archdukes of the country his father had conquered and reconquered.

During those two decades both the emperor and his chancellor, Prince Metternich, realized that their only chance of defeating Napoleon was to let him defeat himself. Francis therefore acquiesced in the many humiliations the upstart emperor visited on a man whose ancestors had been emperors for hundreds of years. Some historians feel that it was Metternich who encouraged Napoleon to believe he had the support of Austria in his fatal march toward Moscow; others, that it was Francis himself; most probably the two men, emperor and chancellor, seeing eye to eye, joined forces to lure Napoleon to his downfall. It came with the Battle of Leipzig in 1813; the following year, Frederick of Prussia and Alexander of Russia entered Paris; Napoleon abdicated and was dispatched to Elba. It was certainly Metternich who exercised a restraining influence when the Treaty of Paris was drawn up: no reparations were demanded, but provisions were made that the "Big Four"—Austria, Prussia, Russia, and England—should meet two months later at Vienna to draw up a "final" map of Europe.

Incredibly enough, during those two decades of war and occupation, Vienna's cultural life glowed with warmth and brilliance. She was still the musical center of the world, and even Napoleon appeared to acknowledge her supremacy, for one of his first acts, when he entered Vienna as her conqueror, had been to command a military guard of honor for Haydn, then in his seventies. The great Mozart had died in 1791, but the excitement generated by that first immemorial trio—Gluck, Haydn, and Mozart—acted like a magnet. In 1794 Beethoven returned to Vienna to live and was soon to be seen at musical evenings at one or another of Vienna's splendid baroque palaces—in particular, the Palais Lobkowitz (where some say his *Eroica* was first performed in 1804) and the Palais Rasumof-

35

sky, the home of the Russian ambassador. *Fidelio*, the musical pro-
clamation of human love and liberty, was first produced at the
Theater an der Wien in 1805, the year of the Battles of Trafalgar
and Austerlitz, the year of the Treaty of Pressburg (by which Austria
lost Tyrol and Venetia) the year of the first French occupation of
Vienna. The following year Francis renounced the crown of the
Holy Roman Empire, but, as he had already assumed that of the
Empire of Austria, he remained an emperor—though one, during
those Napoleonic years, without much of an empire to call his own.

After the defeat of Napoleon, however, he recovered much of
his lost dominions, and Vienna became the chief city of Europe.
During the Congress that resulted from the Treaty of Paris, the
city played host to a more glittering array of monarchs and their
retinues than has probably been seen before or since at any one time
and place. Vienna could not afford the party she was throwing
(the empire was virtually bankrupt), but she did it all the same—
and did it well. There were no complaints from any emperors,
kings, or princes about a dearth of entertainment. The city rocked
with waltz music, operas, and operettas; a fever that was to spread,
and to continue, developing into the popularity of musicals so
evident today throughout the world.

The famous words of the Prince de Ligne, *"Le Congrès danse,
mais ne marche pas,"* were not, however, quite true. The Congress
was dancing, to be sure, but behind the scenes things were getting
done as well. If Metternich, Castlereagh, and Talleyrand carved up
Europe without the slightest regard for national identities, they
also enabled the powers of Europe to live at peace for forty years—
no mean achievement on that contentious continent.

The presence of all these crowned heads with their counsellors and representatives meant that the splendors of Vienna's musical life were destined to be talked about—and perhaps imitated— virtually everywhere in the civilized world. On January 25, 1815, at the Rittersaal of the Hofburg, to celebrate the birthday of the tsarina before an audience of emperors and empresses, kings and queens, and their ministers, Beethoven conducted a concert of his own works and even played the piano himself, accompanying the quartet from *Fidelio*, "*Mir ist so wunderbar*." The Congress ended rather abruptly in 1815 when word arrived that Napoleon had escaped from Elba and was marching on Paris; but the Battle of Waterloo, a short time later, put a second, and final, end to the Corsican's dreams. Europe settled down to enjoy the forty years of peace that the Congress of Vienna had made possible.

The Austrian Empire was eaten, as Metternich and the emperor both realized, with rot, and the only way to keep the house from collapsing was through a system of rigid autocracy. Here again historians differ as to whether the policy, with its implementation, was due to Francis himself or to Metternich; and here again, in all probability, it was due to both acting in concert. Nor did the total absence of political freedom have a dampening effect on the social and cultural life of the capital. Though Vienna's brilliance may have been too dearly bought, as the events of 1848 were to demonstrate, the brilliance was there, and for much of it the world must still remain grateful. Beethoven conquered his deafness and went on working until his death in 1827. The following year Vienna witnessed the untimely death, at thirty-two, of another of her talented sons. Although most Viennese did not consider Schubert to be the genius that Beethoven was, Beethoven himself had recognized his greatness. Just before he died, reading some of

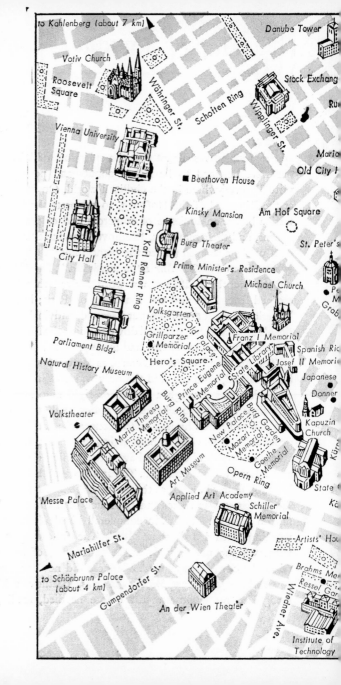

Map of Vienna

Holland St.

Tabor St.

Prater St.

to the Danube (about 2 km)

DANUBE

CANAL

de Cathedral

Jewish Ave.

Fleischmarkt St.

Post Office

Aspern Square

Old University

University Church

Government Bldgs.

Stuben Ring

Mozart House

Museum of Applied Arts

Stephen's Cathedral

Singer St.

Coburg Palace

Railway Station

Francisco Monastery

Schubert Memorial

Bruckner Memorial

Citizens' Park

Schubert Ring, Park Ring

Johann Strauss Memorial

Schwarzenberg Ave.

Kursalon

Beethoven Memorial

Concert House

kvereinsaal

Academy Theater

ienna History Museum

to Central Cemetery and Airport

to Belvedere Palace

rch

VIENNA 🦋

Schubert's songs, sweet, simple works that express the soul of Vienna, Beethoven remarked, "He has the true divine spark."

The luster of these peaceful years—the years between Napoleon and Karl Marx—was not confined to music. In the theater there were Ferdinand Raimund and Johann Nestroy; in art there was what we now call Biedermeir, which symbolized a comfortable and prosperous way of life as well as a style of painting and furniture. The great art collections for which Vienna is famous were steadily being augmented. The Albertina had been founded as far back as 1795; the imperial collection was by now famous all over Europe, and so were some of the collections in the palaces of the aristocracy.

In 1835, with the death of Francis, his son Ferdinand had come to the throne. Although he was subject to fits of insanity, he was not considered ineligible to wear the imperial crown—presumably because Prince Metternich, who was still chancellor, hoped through a weak king to wield the kind of power that he had been denied under Francis. His attempt, however, failed, and during the crucial years between 1836 and 1848 Austria was governed by a coalition of men whose only tie was reciprocal distrust. It was a coalition that satisfied no single group within the ramshackle empire, from aristocrat to peasant, and when the explosion came no one was surprised—not even, in all likelihood, Metternich himself.

He tendered his resignation in March and left at once for England. With his departure, the government sought to woo Vienna back to order by offering such reforms as abolition of press censorship; but it was too late. Rioting continued, and on May 17, 1848, Ferdinand and his court fled to Innsbruck. After a constituent assembly had been formed and had passed the most urgent reforms, Ferdinand returned to Vienna but was unable to remain. Further

40

uprisings forced him to go to Olomouc, in Moravia, and it was there he abdicated in favor of his nephew, Franz Joseph, a new government having meanwhile been formed under Prince Felix Schwarzenberg. Vienna was at length restored to order, and Franz Joseph, who was destined to reign for sixty-eight years, returned to Vienna at the age of eighteen ready to take up the duties that God had thrust upon him—and determined to be the absolute monarch that he believed Habsburgs had the divine right to be.

It was fortunate for Franz Joseph that he possessed this firm conviction; it sustained him through all the sorrows that lay ahead—the deaths and assassinations, the loss of fragments of his beloved empire. The only anguish he was spared was the final one: he died two years before the end of World War I.

And yet, despite the misfortunes of the reign, it was a culturally brilliant one—brilliant enough to be worthy of the title of the second Golden Age of Vienna. Now the aristocratic atmosphere of the Golden Age under Maria Theresa was replaced by a spirit of modernism, socialism, militarism, a popular love of entertainment and academic pursuits. All of the arts and sciences flourished, with the bourgeoisie taking an active part. If the age produced no musical geniuses to equal Mozart and Beethoven, it could boast a collection of composers unrivalled by any other single city of Europe: Brahms, Bruckner, Mahler, and later, Hugo Wolf, Schoenberg and Alban Berg—all active in the Austrian capital within the reign of Franz Joseph. Sigmund Freud pondered the vagaries of man and gave the world his startling conclusions. Arthur Schnitzler, Hugo von Hofmannsthal, Peter Altenberg, Karl Kraus, Robert Musil, and Stefan Zweig produced their brilliant works, written when they were not otherwise engaged sitting around a table in one of Vienna's many coffeehouses. During this time, also, the University of Vienna was attracting the intelligentsia from all over the world. Its art history department could include the name of Dvorák, its sociology department that of Menger; Freud's psychoanalysis also developed there, and Jerineck taught law. People flocked to study under the famous names of Europe.

Within ten years of Franz Joseph's accession, the modernization of Vienna began when the emperor signed a decree providing that the medieval walls of the Innere Stadt be razed. Beyond the walls lay the *glacis*, which, for reasons of defense, had always been kept clear. Here, during the next thirty years, were laid out the great boulevards that compose the Ringstrasse, and here, on either side of the Ring, rose that series of amazing buildings that contribute so much to Vienna's distinctive character. All the buildings, public and private, had a style: Renaissance, Gothic, medieval Flemish, neo-classical. Architects from all over Austria as well as from abroad worked furiously to draw up plans that would please the industrialists and bankers who were financing this huge undertaking.

The new Opera House on the Ring was opened in 1869 with a gala performance of *Don Giovanni*; then came the Museum for the History of Art and the Museum for Natural History; Parliament was Hellenistic in style, while the Musikverein was Renaissance and the Town Hall, Gothic. It was a grandiose project, and the carefully placed statues and monuments, parks and *allées* somehow converted what might have been an impenetrable jungle of styles into a lovely and carefully pruned forest where each element makes its contribution to an imposing whole. Later on, the Secession artists of Vienna (Gustave Klimt, Egon Schiele, O. Kokoschka, Otto

Wagner, and Joseph M. Olbrich) were to have a resounding influence, especially on architecture and design, that would equal that of art nouveau.

In 1879 the twenty-fifth wedding anniversary of the emperor and empress was celebrated with a great pageant that proceeded from Praterstern along the Ringstrasse to the imperial palace, with the two chief celebrants watching from beneath a festive canopy. All the many floats, and indeed all the costumes, had been designed by Hans Markart, a painter who had studied in Venice and who delighted in neo-baroque extravagance. The procession was, in a sense, the apotheosis of Vienna: never again would she shine so brightly, never again would her ruling house make so brave a show. Destiny had other less happy days in store for the Habsburgs.

In 1854 the emperor had married Elizabeth of Bavaria, a beautiful but inexperienced seventeen-year-old princess who was in no way prepared to play the exacting role of empress of Austria; nor was she able to provide the emperor either with the vital spark of imagination that he lacked or with the restraint that he so sorely needed. She did, however, supply him with an heir: Crown Prince Rudolph was born in 1858.

Ten years after his parents' silver wedding anniversary, the crown prince had his famous and fatal last meeting with Baroness Marie Vetsera at his hunting lodge at Mayerling. The next morning, her dead body, covered with flowers, was found beside his; the girl was clandestinely removed and given a secret burial so as to avoid what would have been an even more shattering scandal. Rudolph himself, as though he were not a suicide, was properly buried in Vienna's Capuchin vault. The heir to the throne was now Archduke Franz Ferdinand, the emperor's nephew.

VIENNA 🌱

It seems reasonably clear that the murder and suicide were not the result of unrequited love on either side but rather stemmed from Rudolph's hatred of his own life. His father, treating his son as he treated everyone else, had consistently refused to grant him either independence or authority. It is noteworthy that among the farewell notes Rudolph left, not one word was addressed to his father. His mother, antagonistic to her stern-willed mother-in-law, had grown increasingly estranged from her own family and spent longer and longer periods abroad. It was on one of these occasions that she was stabbed to death by an Italian anarchist in Geneva. The death of this sad, lonely, beautiful woman was a senseless act of hatred, for it had, and could have, no effect whatsoever on the autocratic policies of the emperor.

It was the third in a chain of violent deaths that touched Franz Joseph intimately—but it was not the last. The first was the execution of his younger brother, Maximilian, by a Mexican firing squad; the second, the suicide of his son; the third, the killing of his wife; and the fourth, the assassination of his nephew at Sarajevo on June 28, 1914. The emperor, at the head of a disintegrating empire, could not free himself from the ties that bound him to Germany, whose head of state was determined on war. Franz Joseph found himself and his country embroiled in a war he had ardently hoped to avoid; had he been an abler or more astute man, he might have succeeded. Fortunately for him, he died in 1916, before the ignominy of defeat and the total dissolution of his empire.

The new emperor reigned for just two years before, in November, 1918, he stated, "I hereby renounce all part in conducting the business of the State." The last Habsburg emperor left Vienna, which now found herself the capital of a small republic of seven million inhabitants. The scattered possessions of the empire vanished into other nations' pockets, or became independent nations; Austria, in Clemenceau's phrase, was what was left.

Conditions in Vienna were dreadful after the war's end. There was not enough food to feed the people who were already there, and more kept pouring in, demobilized soldiers and civil servants who had formerly administered the far-flung empire. There were no jobs, and the terrible specter of inflation loomed ever larger; money was virtually worthless. The city that had once been the capital of Europe now became a soup kitchen, her citizens subsisting mournfully on charity from abroad.

The history of Vienna between 1918 and 1938 is not a particularly happy one, despite some constructive moments. There was much political squabbling and jockeying for power, apprehension about the future, fear of both Germany and Russia. At the same time, thanks to a Socialist majority in the city's administration, much was accomplished. Sixty thousand new flats for workers were built, medical services were expanded, schools and hospitals were built, highways were laid down, industry was given much-needed encouragement. A great deal of this activity was financed by a loan made through the League of Nations.

The Austrian economy seemed, for a time, to be stabilizing itself. Then, in 1931, came the failure of the Creditanstalt Bank. Shortly thereafter, with the whole world in the throes of economic depression, Austrians began to hear how prosperous Germany was growing under Hitler. Engelbert Dollfuss, who became chancellor in 1932, soon found himself threatened by Hitler on one side and Mussolini on the other, with growing Bolshevik power on still a third. Dollfuss leaned toward Mussolini, but Hilter had no inten-

tion of loosening his grasp on the small, economically fragile republic. The campaign he waged increased steadily in violence. Brief
civil war in Vienna was followed by the Nazi assassination of Dollfuss and the inauguration of Kurt Schuschnigg as chancellor.

But he was unable to withstand the growing might and fury
of Hitler coupled with the curious apathy of the Western democra-
cies. On March 13, 1931, Hitler entered Vienna, and Austria slipped
into the cesspool of Nazi-occupied countries. With Hitler's entry, and
also for a short time before and after, the mass exodus of Jews from
the city was taking place. Vienna lost many of her most eminent
musicians, artists, and intellectuals. Most of them headed west, to
establish themselves in England and America, thus spreading Viennese culture to new areas.

With her liberation, in April, 1945, the country and her capital
were divided into four zones, Soviet, American, British, and French.
The Innere Stadt was to be controlled by all four powers. The
flag atop the imperial palace and the guards before it changed week
by week as the four assumed their responsibilities in turn. Conditions in the capital were pitiful. Food was extremely scarce, and
Austrian money valueless to buy it; power cuts were frequent, and
there was almost no transportation. Three of the city's chief symbols
had been gutted by fire and bombs: the Opera, the Burgtheater,
and St. Stephen's Cathedral.

Would Vienna ever recover? Strangely, Vienna being Vienna,
the recovery began to take effect almost immediately. Even before
the German surrender, the philharmonic gave a concert, the opera
gave a performance in the undamaged Volksoper, and the theaters that were still usable announced their opening productions.
Gradually the political situation grew stable once again, and so

also, thanks to the Marshall Plan, did the Austrian economy. Soviet intransigence delayed the long-desired State Treaty until May 15, 1955. To the people of Vienna who thronged the Belvedere gardens, where the treaty was signed by the foreign ministers of the four powers and of Austria, the sight of the document as the foreign minister held it aloft was like a shot in the arm. Vienna was herself again.

In 1955 also, the Spanish Riding School and the Burgtheater were reopened, and in November of that year came the gala premiere of the rebuilt opera. A seat in the orchestra cost up to two hundred dollars. Three years earlier, the great bell of St. Stephen's, the Pummerin, which had been cast originally out of Turkish cannon captured in 1711, was recast and returned in a grand procession to its original home. Within a decade, the great symbols of Vienna had risen from the rubble of war—and if Austria has her way, they will never fall again, for she has adopted a policy of strict neutrality.

Even if the empire is gone, and Austria is only a very small country today, the Viennese are leading their lives much as they did before. They still thrive on their coffee, wine, music, and theater, and they still have the same character—pessimistic and sentimental on the surface, but gentle and good-humored underneath. They have seen their life and culture become known to the world through art, music, theater, politics, and even motion pictures, such as *The Congress Dances*, *The Love of Mayerling*, *Masquerade* and *Burgtheater*. They can also enjoy the role their city has reassumed as a meeting place between East and West—as demonstrated by the famous conference between John F. Kennedy and Nikita Khrushchev, and the fact that the offices of the International Atomic Energy Agency are located in Vienna.

(The following genealogies show the relationship between the people mentioned in the text. Dotted lines indicate omissions from the complete genealogy)

HOUSE OF BABENBURG

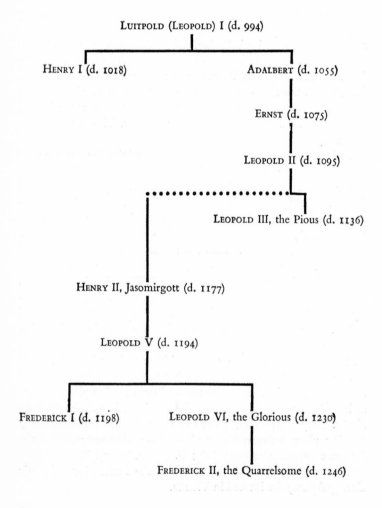

HOUSE OF HABSBURG

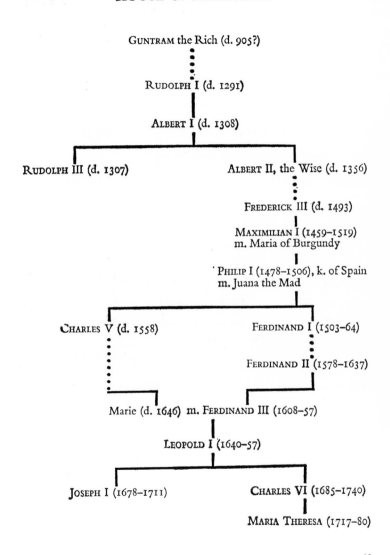

GUNTRAM the Rich (d. 905?)

RUDOLPH I (d. 1291)

ALBERT I (d. 1308)

RUDOLPH III (d. 1307)

ALBERT II, the Wise (d. 1356)

FREDERICK III (d. 1493)

MAXIMILIAN I (1459–1519)
m. Maria of Burgundy

PHILIP I (1478–1506), k. of Spain
m. Juana the Mad

CHARLES V (d. 1558)

FERDINAND I (1503–64)

FERDINAND II (1578–1637)

Marie (d. 1646) m. FERDINAND III (1608–57)

LEOPOLD I (1640–57)

JOSEPH I (1678–1711)

CHARLES VI (1685–1740)

MARIA THERESA (1717–80)

HOUSE OF HABSBURG-LORRAINE

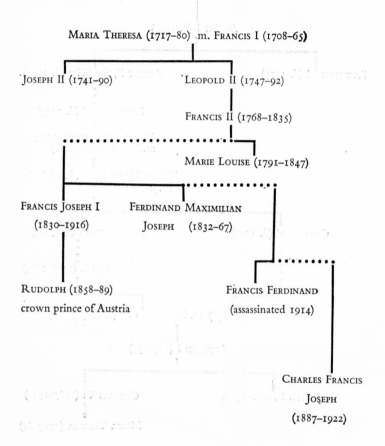

MARIA THERESA (1717–80) m. FRANCIS I (1708–65)

JOSEPH II (1741–90)   LEOPOLD II (1747–92)

FRANCIS II (1768–1835)

MARIE LOUISE (1791–1847)

FRANCIS JOSEPH I   FERDINAND MAXIMILIAN
(1830–1916)   JOSEPH (1832–67)

RUDOLPH (1858–89)   FRANCIS FERDINAND
crown prince of Austria   (assassinated 1914)

CHARLES FRANCIS
JOSEPH
(1887–1922)

6. *Sitting in the sun* is a favorite occupation in Vienna, which does not enjoy an overabundance of sunlight the year round; further, many of the old houses are dark, so outside is the place to be when the sun shines.

7. *Kärntnerstrasse,* which leads from the Opera House to St. Stephen's, is a broad, busy, fashionable thoroughfare, with some of the city's best hotels and stores as well as cafes, travel offices, and the like.

52

8. *Votivkirche* was built by architect Heinrich Ferstel to commemorate Emperor Franz Joseph's surviving an assassination attempt in 1853.

9. *Burgtor* ("Palace Gate") opens onto the Michaelerplatz. Haydn once lived nearby, as did Chopin briefly.

◄10. *Zentralfriedhof* (*overleaf*) is the final resting place for many of Austria's statesmen, scholars and composers. Memorial in center is dedicated to Mozart.

11. *Bride and groom* descending the steps of the Karlskirche, one of Vienna's major baroque monuments, completed in 1737.

12. *Ringstrasse,* shown here in early morning, is shaped rather like a horseshoe, with the Danube Canal at its open end: thus the Innere Stadt, the ancient heart of Vienna, is entirely enclosed by the canal and the various boulevards that make up the Ring. Construction of the Ring was begun in 1856, eight years after the accession of Franz Joseph, on the site of the *glacis* (or defensive open spaces) that surrounded the old walls of the city. Between 1856 and 1890, the great tree-shaded avenues were laid out, with their parks, gardens, and monuments, and the many public buildings that line the Ring were constructed in imitation of former styles (Hellenistic, Romanesque, Gothic), and if some of the buildings seem pompous or even absurd by the more austere standards of our own day, taken together, with the gardens that surround them, they form a unique architectural complex. Vienna would not be Vienna without her Ringstrasse.

14. *Burgtheater,* also on the Ring, gave its opening performance in 1888, but architecturally it was found to be defective in so many ways (from some of the boxes one could not see the stage) it had to be rebuilt in 1897.

◀ 13. *Staatsoper (overleaf),* on the Opernring, a somewhat sentimentalized version of the Renaissance, opened the the night of May 25, 1869, with a gala performance of *Don Giovanni*; both the emperor and the king of Hanover were in the audience.

15. *Posters* announcing recitals, concerts, operas galore give proof that Vienna is still the "City of Music"—and also of the other arts, as a study of the posters suggests.

16. *Outdoor concerts* are given on warm summer evenings in the Stadtpark (also on the Ring), and the music is likely to be one of Strauss's familiar waltzes—so familiar, perhaps, that the two ladies in the foreground seem to be more interested in their gossip.

63

17. *Gesellschaft der Musikfreunde* makes its home here and gives the building its official name, but Viennese call it simply the Musikverein. Pictured here is the ornate and gilded Grosser Musikvereinsaal, where the Vienna Philharmonic gives regular concerts.

18. *Musikverein* has two other halls, one for recitals and one for chamber music, as well as a collection of old musical instruments. It also houses a music publisher and a piano maker.

19. *Volksoper* is one of only two theaters left in Vienna that perform the saccharine, improbable operettas that were once so popular. In the 1880's there were six.

20. *Wiener Konzerthaus,* like the Musikverein, has three halls—a large one for full orchestral performances and two smaller ones, the Mozartsaal and the Schubertsaal.

21.   *Heldendenkmal,* on the Burgring, commemorates the Battle of Leipzig, fought between October 16 and 19, 1813, which saw the destruction of Napoleon and his *grande armée.* One of the most crucial events of modern European history, the battle was waged between Napoleon on one side and the Austrian army, led by Prince Schwarzenberg, with the Prussian army, led by Prince von Blücher, on the other. Schwarzenberg appears to have been an indifferent commander, but when on October 18 he received the support of the Swedish army under Bernadotte, Napoleon's doom was sealed; and Schwarzenberg, as a result, was handsomely rewarded. He became one of the heroes (*Helden*) toward whom the imperial government of Austria felt itself especially indebted. (See Plates 23 and 24.)

22. *Alte Hofburg* stands on the site where Habsburgs lived and ruled from the time Count Rudolph defeated Ottakar, King of Bohemia, at Marchfeld in the thirteenth century until 1918, when the last Habsburg emperor, the grandson of Franz Joseph, abdicated.

23. *Francis* was the last of the Holy ▶ Roman emperors, and as such was Francis II, but two years before he renounced the title, putting an end to the Holy Roman Empire, he had assumed the title of hereditary emperor of Austria, as Francis I. His name crowns the Heldendenkmal.

AMOREM · MEVM · POPVLIS · MEIS

24. *Prince Eugene of Savoy* is another of Austria's *Helden*, for he was among the most courageous of officers who served under Duke Charles of Lorraine in lifting the Turkish siege of Vienna in 1683. He fought hard and valiantly in the service of the Habsburgs, and in 1717 took Belgrade from the Turks. Behind Prince Eugene rises the imposing, late nineteenth-century façade of the New Burg.

25. *Spanish Riding School,* in the baroque manège of the Hofburg, is one of the sights of Vienna. Here, beneath elegant chandeliers, white stallions perform intricate steps to Mozart's music; the horses are called Lipizzaner because, until 1918, the stud farm was located at Lipizza (near Trieste).

26. *Twenty-story building,* on the banks ▶ of the Danube, sports a sixty-foot tower that tells Viennese every night what tomorrow's weather is likely to be: a yellow light means fair; white, cloudy; blue, rain; and red, storms.

27—29. *Wiener Sänger-knaben*—Vienna Choir-boys — are another Habsburg inheritance. Toscanini described them as "voices of angels." There are actually three choirs, two of which are usually abroad, giving performances, while the third sings every Sunday at mass at the Hofburg-kapelle. They make their headquarters at the Augarten Palais.

31—33. *First church* of St. Stephen, built in the twelfth century, was a parish church. After its destruction by fire, King Ottakar of Bohemia, who had occupied Vienna, began the construction of a new Romanesque church in 1259. The church became a cathedral in 1469, during the reign of Frederick III. Brutally damaged by bombs in August, 1945, the church has now been completely restored, and the great bell has been reinstalled. The roof, a section of which is shown in Plate 31, is composed of 250,000 enamelled tiles from Bohemia. The splendid pulpit in Plate 32 is the work of Anton Pilgram and dates from the early sixteenth century. In the panoramic view above, the church on the left is St. Peter's, built in the eighteenth century.

34. *Outdoor stalls* are a popular Viennese institution. Below are shown a few of the souvenir stalls clustered alongside the main gate of St. Stephen's. During the night, after restaurants close, people flock to stalls that sell rich boiled sausages served in rolls. The sausage is one of the delights of Vienna.

35. *Abbey of Heiligenkreuz* is one of the handsomest of the courts built in Vienna in ancient times by the rich monasteries and abbeys of Lower Austria. Heiligenkreuz shows traces of Romanesque and Gothic as well as baroque. Monument in foreground commemorates the victims of the plague.

36. *Franziskanerkirche* was built in the fourteenth century and restored at the beginning of the seventeenth.

38. *Hofburg gate* was built in the 1880's after designs by the great baroque architect, Fischer von Erlach. (See Plate 22.)

37. *Gluck,* though born a German, spent much of his time in Vienna, where he lived not far from the Karlskirche. This memorial to the composer of *Orfeo e Euridice* stands beside the church.

39. *Maria Theresa* sits as firmly atop this statue in her honor as she sat on the throne of Austria for forty years; below her are grouped the leading military figures of her reign as well as scholars and musicians, including the child Mozart (who was presented to her when he was six years old).

40. *Museum for the History of Art,* built by Gootfried Semper and Karl Hasenauer and completed in 1881 as part of the Ring reconstruction, houses the tremendous Habsburg art collection and ranks among the greatest museums of the world.

42. *Crown* belonging to the Museum is thought to have been that used in the coronation of Otto the Great in Rome as first Holy Roman emperor.

◀41. *Breughels (overleaf)* in the Museum's collection number some fifteen —about half of all that have survived!

43.   *Franz Joseph Haydn* was born in 1732 in a village in Lower Austria, on the Hungarian border, of a family that was probably of Croatian stock. When he was eight years old, he entered the choir of St. Stephen's in Vienna, and he was destined to spend most of the rest of his life in and around Vienna. For thirty years—from 1760 to 1790—he lived under the protection of the Esterhazys. His last years were spent in the house shown below, which is now the Haydn Museum. There he composed his last eight *Masses*, his last chamber music, the Austrian national anthem, the *Creation*, and the *Seasons*. No city in the world can compete with Vienna in the number of monuments, museums, houses, theaters, concert halls, and churches intimately associated with the great composers of the Golden Age.

44. *Mozart* was born in Salzburg and traveled
widely across Europe during the short span of his
life, but Vienna claims him for her own. Though
she did not, during his lifetime, grant him the
honors he so richly deserved, she has been trying
to atone for it every since. This splendid memorial
in the Burggarten, erected in 1905, is but one of
her efforts in that direction.

45. *Restored* in 1962, the Theater an der Wien gave its first performance in 1801 and has seen the first nights not only of *Fidelio* but also of Beethoven's Fifth and Sixth Symphonies.

46. *Death of Mozart* is shrouded in mystery: not only the cause of his early death but the actual place where he was buried. This memorial is on the presumed site of his grave.

47—48. *Beethoven*, another "foreigner," has also been adopted by Vienna, and indeed he himself preferred the city to all others. On the third floor of the building shown below, on Mölkerbastei, he is said to have spent some ten years and written three of his nine symphonies. The monument (opposite) is in Beethovenplatz.

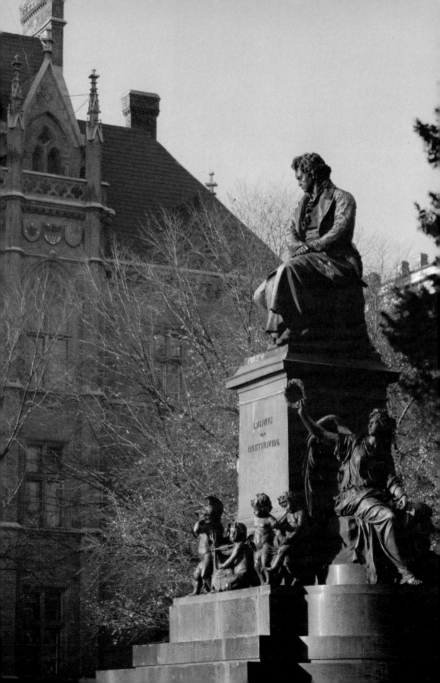

49—50. *Franz Schubert,* a native son of Vienna, is intimately associated with the city and her people—although he, too, during his lifetime, suffered from their neglect. Many years were spent in penury, and it is doubtful if he would have survived but for the generosity of his friends. The monument on the left stands in Vienna's Stadtpark; below is the wine garden outside Vienna with the famous linden tree about which Schubert wrote one of his loveliest songs.

51—52. *Composer* of much highly regarded symphonic music, Schubert is still best known for his lieder—and best loved for them by his fellow citizens. They have estalished two museums in his honor (that shown above is the house where he was born), and they have erected a statue of Goethe in the Opernring in recognition of the fact that Schubert set seventy-two of Goethe's poems to music.

53. *Staatsoper (overleaf)* is on the left in this photograph of busy Kärntner-strasse as it heads toward St. Stephen's. Beneath the arches are entrances to the Opera's dressing rooms.

55. *Rathaus,* or Town Hall, was designed by its architect, Friedrich Schmidt, to suggest the imposing Gothic town halls of Belgium. It opened its doors in 1883.

54. *Burgtheater,* seen here from the lovely, flower-strewn Volksgarten, is one of the Ring buildings: it held its first performance on October 14, 1888. Found to be unsatisfactory, it was rebuilt ten years later.

98

56. *Vienna University*, founded in 1365, is the oldest German-speaking university in existence, though it must yield to its elder sisters in Prague (1348) and Cracow (1364), at both of which German was once the official language. The present Italianate building, inaugurated in 1883, lies on Dr. Karl Lueger-Ring, just where the Ring turns to head back toward the Danube Canal.

57. *Schottentor,* with Votivkirche.

58. *Campus* of Vienna University.

59. *Rooseveltplatz* (formerly Hitlerplatz).

60. *Volksgarten*, with Rathaus in background.

61—62. *Schönbrunn* and the Belvedere are monuments to Vienna's two great baroque architects—Fischer von Erlach and Lucas von Hildebrandt—although Schönbrunn as it now stands is considerably less grandiose than the architect's original conception and owes as much to Fischer's son and to Nikolaus Paccassi as to Fischer himself. The Habsburg hunting lodge that stood on the present site of Schönbrunn was completely destroyed by the Turks, and Fischer planned to make the new palace a rival to Versailles; but though the Habsburgs declined to be so extravagant as the Bourbons, Schönbrunn remains a splendid monument to the architect's genius. The Upper and Lower Belvedere were built for Prince Eugene of Savoy, the hero of the war against the Turks. Belvedere, a favorite with children, is shown below; opposite is a section of Schönbrunn's gardens.

63. *Front view* of Belvedere Palace

64. *View of Vienna* from the Belvedere gardens.

65.   *Badly damaged* by bombs during the war,
as well as by Nazi vandalism before the war,
and occupied by the British element of the
Allied High Commission after 1945, Schönbrunn has now been magnificently restored
—as this resplendent gallery proves.

66. *One wonders* how many rooms Fischer von Erlach's original plans called for, for the economy version that was finally produced consists of twelve hundred of them! Of the forty-five that are open to the public, the one shown below is that in which Franz Joseph was born and died.

67. *Front view* of Schönbrunn Palace.

68. *Gloriette* in background is where Fischer von Erlach originally envisaged placing the stupendous palace he wanted to build for the future emperor Joseph I. The present-day visitor to Vienna may regret that the place was never built, but he can hardly regret the formal beauty of Schönbrunn's gardens.

69. *Volksgarten's* flowers are often transplanted there from hothouses, so that the park is never bare, never without color and scent to soothe nerves irritated by the noisy and busy streets nearby. Below, a gardener is trimming the Volksgarten's rose bushes. In the park are statues both of Vienna's greatest dramatic poet, Franz Grillparzer, many of whose plays preached the thesis that wordly ambition is pointless, and—appropriately enough—of the unhappy Empress Elizabeth, considered to be the most beautiful woman in Europe, who was stabbed to death by an assassin in as useless an act as any in history.

70. *Naschmarkt,* Vienna's largest market, is in the center of town, only a few minutes' walk from the Opera. There are some two hundred stores in the market, affording the buyer a wide choice of goods; prices are usually cheaper than elsewhere.

71. *Theaterkarten,* says the sign on the Kärntnerstrasse, and the theatre tickets are displayed right in the shop window. The broker charges only a twenty percent commission—not as in New York, where the sky's the limit.

72. *Vienna's pastry shops (overleaf)* ▶
are world-famous, and deservedly so.
Demel's, nearly two hundred years old,
is much the same as it was when Emperor Franz Joseph sent in for some
Faschingskrapfen, while Sacher—so the
story goes—invented its famous tart
on orders from Metternich for the
Congress of Vienna.

73. *Viennese women* are dressier than their American or English cousins, and they have a wide choice of places to shop, including the ubiquitous Palmers, which is to be found all over the city.

74. *Eduard Sacher,* a well-known chef, opened his hotel right behind the Opera in 1876, just seven years after the building was completed.

75. *Fiakers* may still be hired in front of St. Stephen's or the Opera, but this agreeable means of transportation is fast disappearing.

76. *Lovely Austrian girls* still favor the native *dirndl* costume, a charming dress with apron, for both city and country wear.

77. *Burggarten,* in wintertime, is a fine place to come and soak in the sun.

78. *Children*, playing in one of Vienna's parks, are like children anywhere—but they seem more polite and courteous, perhaps because of the Habsburg heritage.

79. *Paulus Stube,* one of the city's
better-known wine taverns, started
out in life long ago as the wine cellar
of a monastery; music is typical
Viennese Schrammel.

80. *Wine drinking* is a characteristic ▶
Viennese way to relax of an evening—
thanks to the Romans, who first im-
ported the grape to Austria two thousand years ago.

81. *Clock* at Hoher Markt marks the former center of the ancient city; the market stands on a hill sloping down to the Danube Canal.

82. *Pestsäule* (Plague Memorial) commemorates Vienna's thanksgiving at the end of the great plague of 1679; master designer was Fischer von Erlach.

83. *Georg Raphael Donner,* Austria's most illustrious baroque sculptor, was commissioned in 1737 to do a fountain in the Neuer Markt symbolizing the four great rivers of Austria surmounted by a figure of Providence (said to have been modeled after the sculptor's wife).

84. *Buying flowers* to decorate a grave at the Zentralfriedhof: both buyer and seller seem reasonably cheerful. Opposite (Plates 85–90) are shown the graves of some of Austria's great composers.

91. *Statue of Brahms* in the Ressel-park, near Karlskirche and not far from where the great composer died.

92. *Stadtpark* is the appropriate setting for the statue of Johann Strauss (shown on the front cover), with a marble frame symbolizing the Danube. The sculptor was Edmund Hellmer; the statue was unveiled in 1923.

93. *Opera Ball* is the grand climax of the winter season, although Vienna has hundreds of balls that are not quite so formal—but perhaps even more fun.

94. *"Wien, Wien, nur du allein"*—the tourist will not be in Vienna long before he hears the familiar but delightful melody and feels the genuine fervor with which it is sung.

96. *Onion-shaped domes* are a common sight in the streets of Vienna; those shown opposite belong to the Allerheilige Dreifaltigkeitskirche, in Alserstrasse, where Beethoven's funeral took place.

95. *Cafe Mozart,* on Albertinaplatz, will be familiar to anyone who saw *The Third Man*; it is a favorite place for an outdoor lunch in summer or a snack at night.

97. *Petit point* is a popular export item that helps bolster the Austrian economy; some three to four thousand women are employed making the kind of embroidery shown above, mostly exported to the United States. Austria is famous also for its handmade blouses, leather goods, and porcelain.

98. *Felder House,* not far from the Rathaus, is the home of the International Industry Development Organization, inaugurated in 1967, which currently employs a staff of four hundred people from forty-seven countries. The fact that the government has spent some five hundred million schillings building a new headquarters for the organization suggests that Austria is taking seriously its role as a link between East and West and hopes to make its declaration of neutrality an emphatic force for world peace in the future.

99. *International Atomic Energy Agency* (IAEA) gives further proof that Vienna, despite the small population of the country, is still very much an international capital.

100. *After the war,* the government inaugurated a number of welfare institutions, among them the children's home shown below.

101. *May Day festivities* ▶ in front of the Rathaus.

102—103. *Prater,* a great park on both the Danube and the Danube Canal, is only a short ride from the center of the city. Formerly a hunting ground for the imperial family, it was the site of the world exposition of 1873, after which it became Vienna's playground, with taverns, cafes, dance halls, a swimming pool, golf course, and so on. Below, children watch a sidewalk artist; opposite, the giant ferris wheel used so effectively in *The Third Man.*

105. *Beethoven Gang* is the name given to this path in the Viennese suburb of Heiligenstadt, where Beethoven spent much time and where, so it is said, he drew from the stream flowing beside the path the motif for the second movement of the *Pastoral* Symphony.

104. *Wienerwald,* a huge forest on the outskirts of the city, is best known in English as the Vienna Woods, from which Johann Strauss drew his *Tales.* Until the mid-nineteenth century, Vienna was almost completely surrounded by forest and there were virtually no suburbs at all, but with the building of the Ring, the city began to expand. The Wienerwald, however, despite the encroachments of the city, has happily retained much of its original, unspoiled beauty.

106—108. *House,* above, one of the many places
where Beethoven lived during his life in Vienna,
has become particularly well known because it
is so characteristic of a country house of the
period. It is in Pfarrplatz, Heiligenstadt. Opposite, the lower plate shows another house where
Beethoven lived, also in Heiligenstadt, and where
he wrote his will. The upper plate opposite shows
the statue of Beethoven that stands in Heiligenstadt Park.

109. *Grinzing*, a wine suburb of Vienna.

110. *Drinking new wine* at a "Heuriger."

111. *Vienna,* as seen from Kahlenberg.

112. *Population* of Vienna is over 1,600,000 (almost a quarter of the total population of the country), and the city, unable to expand any further to south and west, is now spilling over to the left bank of the Danube. Despite all the new construction, however, there are still country inns within easy reach, where Viennese can go to drink new wine and sing their favorite songs to the accompaniment of an accordion.

113. *Benedictine abbey* at Melk, on the right bank of the Danube, is the largest in lower Austria. Built originally as a fort in the tenth century by the Babenbergs, it was given to the Benedictines a couple of centuries later. The present construction, breathtaking in its elegance and daring, dates from the eighteenth century and is the work of Jakob Prandtauer. It is one of the most beautiful baroque churches in all of Austria—and, indeed, in all the world.